Through My Telescope

Heather Rau

ROSEN COMMON CORE READERS

Rosen Classroom™

New York

Published in 2014 by The Rosen Publishing Group, Inc.
29 East 21st Street, New York, NY 10010

Book Design: Mickey Harmon

Photo Credits: Cover Neung Stocker Photography/Shutterstock.com; pp. 3–24 (background) AZP Worldwide/ Shutterstock.com; pp. 5, 7 (girl) Yuri Acurs/Shutterstock.com; p. 7 (sunflower) Steshkin Yevgeniy/Shutterstock.com; p. 9 (mirror) Atiketta Sangasaeng/Shutterstock.com; p. 9 (glass with pencil) leonello calvetti/Shutterstock.com; p. 11 artiomp/ Shutterstock.com; p. 13 Hemera/Thinkstock.com; p. 15 Marek Walisiewicz/Dorling Kindersley/Getty Images; p. 17 Frank Whitney/The Image Bank/Getty Images; p. 19 Cameran Ashraf/Flickr Open/Getty Images; p. 21 JesseChilders/ Shutterstock.com; p. 22 (world map) jcsmilly/Shutterstock.com.

ISBN: 978-1-4777-2617-4
6-pack ISBN: 978-1-4777-2618-1

Manufactured in the United States of America

CPSIA Compliance Information: Batch #CS13RC: For further information contact Rosen Publishing, New York, New York at 1-800-237-9932.

Contents

A New Telescope!

My dad bought me a telescope for my birthday! There are many things I want to do with my telescope. I want to use it to see things that are far away, such as buildings and animals. I also want to use it to see faraway things in the night sky, such as stars, **comets**, planets, and the moon.

First, I want to learn how my telescope works. Telescopes are tools that help people see things that are far away. They do this by **magnifying** objects.

My dad knows a lot about telescopes. Today, he's going to teach me how they work!

Light and Sight

Since telescopes help people see faraway objects, I need to learn all about eyesight. My dad says eyesight is possible because of light. Most natural light comes to Earth from the sun. It travels in waves from the sun and allows us to see.

When light hits an object, some of the light reflects, or bounces back. When I look at an object, the reflected light hits my eyes. My eyes take in the light and send that information to my brain. Then, my brain makes a picture!

This is how eyesight works. It all starts with light!

sun
light

I know there are two types of telescopes, called reflecting and refracting. Reflection is when light bounces off an object. If the object's surface is smooth, like a mirror, light will reflect evenly. That's why you can see your reflection in a mirror. If an object's surface is rough, the light reflects unevenly.

Refraction is when light changes speed and seems to "bend." This happens when light moves through the border between **mediums**. Air, water, and glass are different mediums. When light passes from air to glass or water, it slows down and changes direction.

Reflecting telescopes use mirrors, while refracting telescopes use glass. I'll learn more about how they work soon!

refracting light

reflecting light

Refracting Telescopes

Refracting telescopes use glass lenses to bend light. When light passes through the border between the air and the lens, it bends. Lenses are used in glasses, too. My mom wears glasses, and her lenses refract light in a way that corrects her eyesight.

Lenses are shaped to bend light a certain way. Some, called concave lenses, curve in. When a concave lens collects light, it makes the light spread out. Convex lenses curve out. These lenses bend light toward a single point, called a focal point.

The first telescopes had a combination of concave and convex lenses. Many of the telescopes we use today have two convex lenses.

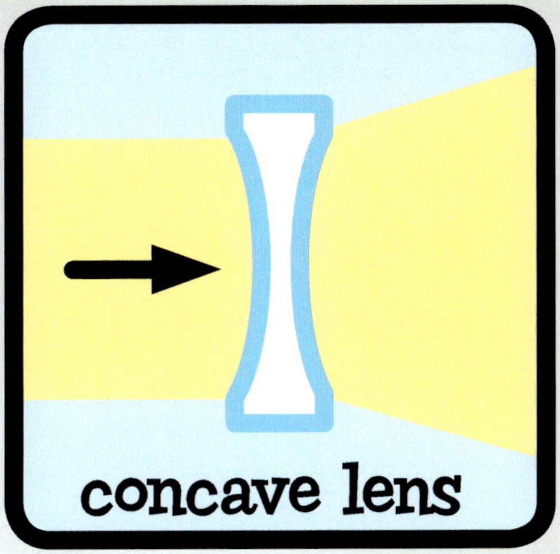

concave lens

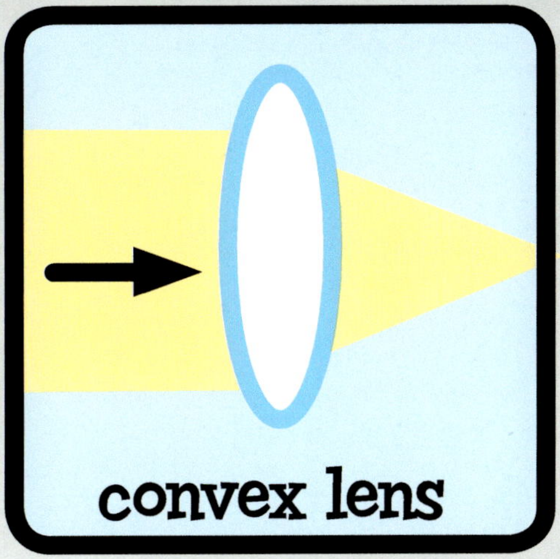

convex lens

My dad says all telescopes work by collecting light and making a distant image seem bigger on the "screen" of your eye. A squirrel in the distance only takes up a tiny part of your eye's screen. If you use a telescope, the squirrel takes up more of the eye's screen.

My dad has a refracting telescope. Refracting telescopes first gather light through a big convex lens in front. The convex lens bends the light and brings it to a focal point. Then, light passes through the eyepiece, which can be concave or convex. Convex eyepieces give a brighter image, but the image is upside down.

Light enters at the main convex lens, meets at a focal point, and then travels through the eyepiece.

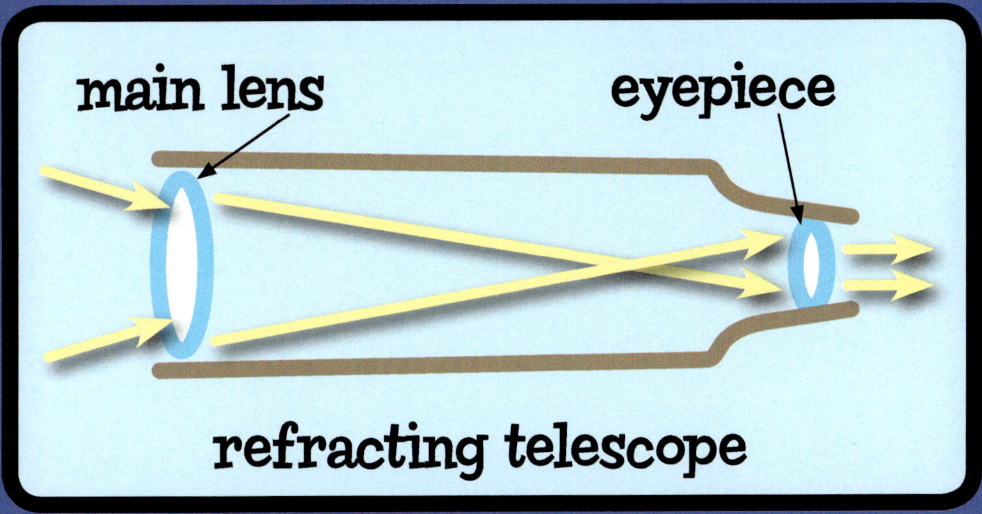
main lens
eyepiece
refracting telescope

Reflecting Telescopes

My dad says refracting telescopes were created before reflecting telescopes. While refracting telescopes were invented in 1608, reflecting ones were invented in 1663. Reflecting telescopes make clearer images and can be used in the dark.

My telescope is a reflecting telescope, which uses mirrors. In a reflecting telescope, light travels through the tube and hits a **primary** mirror, which is concave. This focuses light and reflects it to a secondary mirror. Then the image is sent to a lens in the eyepiece, which magnifies it.

Reflecting telescopes make it possible to see dark objects, or objects that look dim because they're far away. That's why they're good for looking at stars!

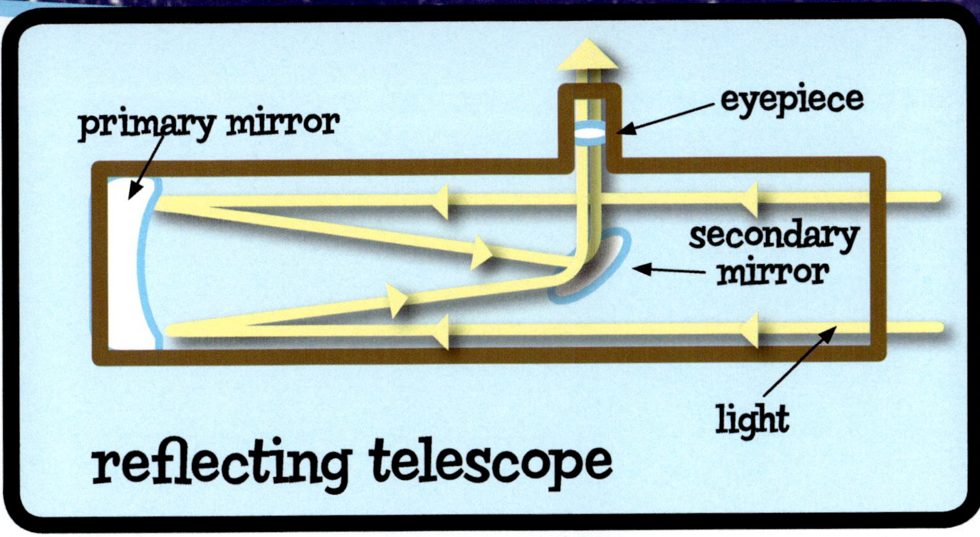

reflecting telescope

My dad says telescopes are judged by how well they collect light and how big they can magnify an image. The bigger a telescope's primary lens or mirror, the more light it collects. The more light it collects, the brighter and clearer the image will be. A handheld telescope has a small lens. It collects less light than a big telescope and shows a dimmer image of faraway objects.

Magnification depends on the length of the telescope and the length of the eyepiece. A longer telescope with a shorter eyepiece gives the best magnification.

The Hubble Space Telescope is 43.5 feet (13.3 m) long, and its primary mirror is 94.5 inches (2.4 m) across! It orbits Earth and takes pictures of faraway space objects.

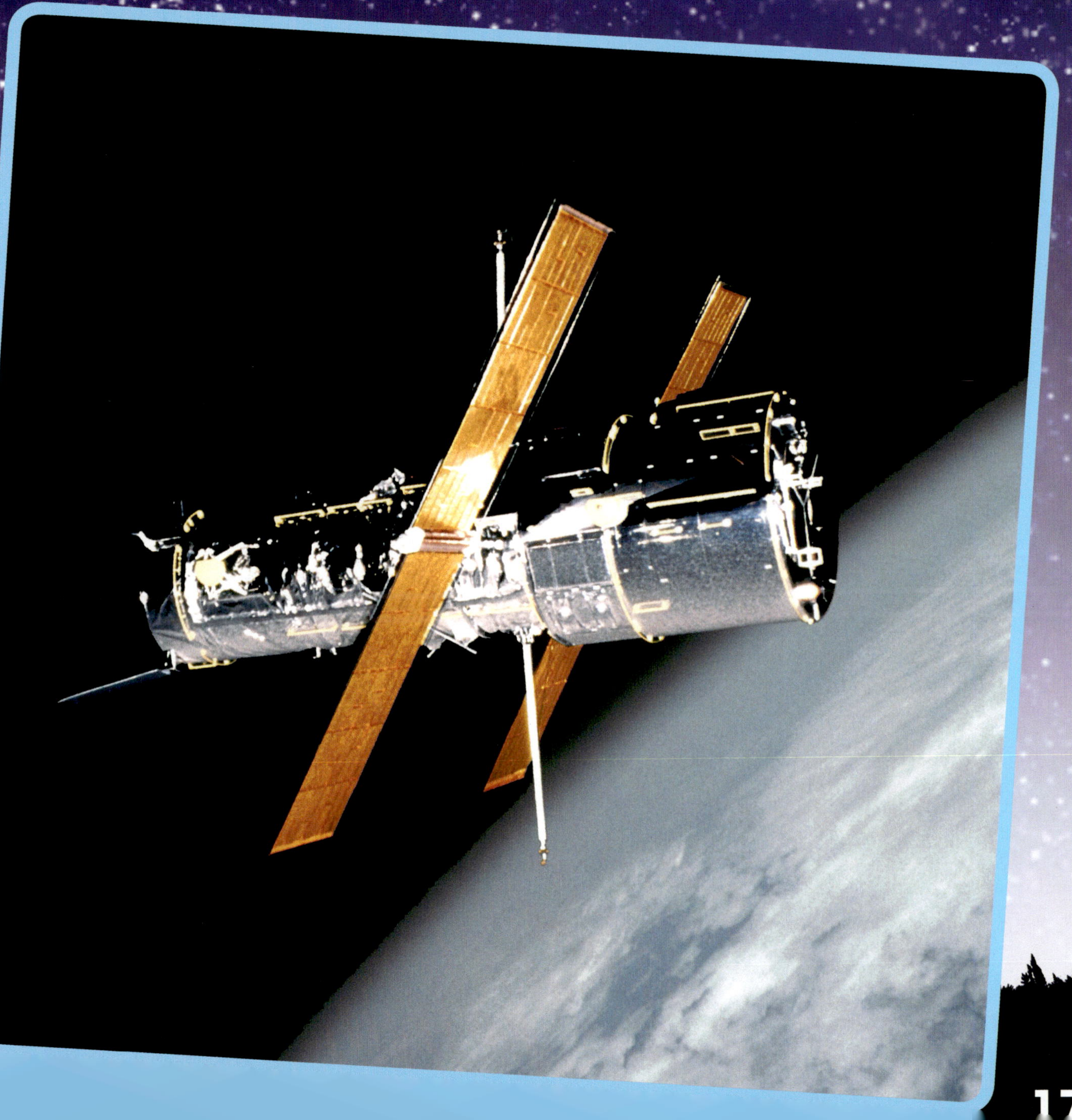

Looking Up

Now that I know how telescopes work, it's time to take mine outside! My dad says it's best to look at brighter objects when you're just starting to use a telescope. They're easier to find. I point my telescope at the moon. I can see many craters that are too small to see with just my eyes.

Next, I point my telescope toward Jupiter, which is usually the easiest planet to see. My telescope is strong enough to see the four biggest moons that circle Jupiter, too!

My dad says one of the most fun things to do with a telescope is to study space. Some objects are hard to find, but some, such as the moon, are easy!

I could see even more things if I had a bigger telescope. The biggest telescopes used to study space are called **observatories**. The Hubble Space Telescope collects light from billions of **light-years** away! There are huge observatories on Earth, too. Observatories make new discoveries about space all the time. My dad says he'll take me to an observatory soon!

I learned that telescopes are very important tools in science. They make it possible to see things that are very far away. They're also lots of fun!

The Griffith Observatory in Los Angeles is a great place to visit to learn more about telescopes and space!

World's Most Powerful Telescopes!

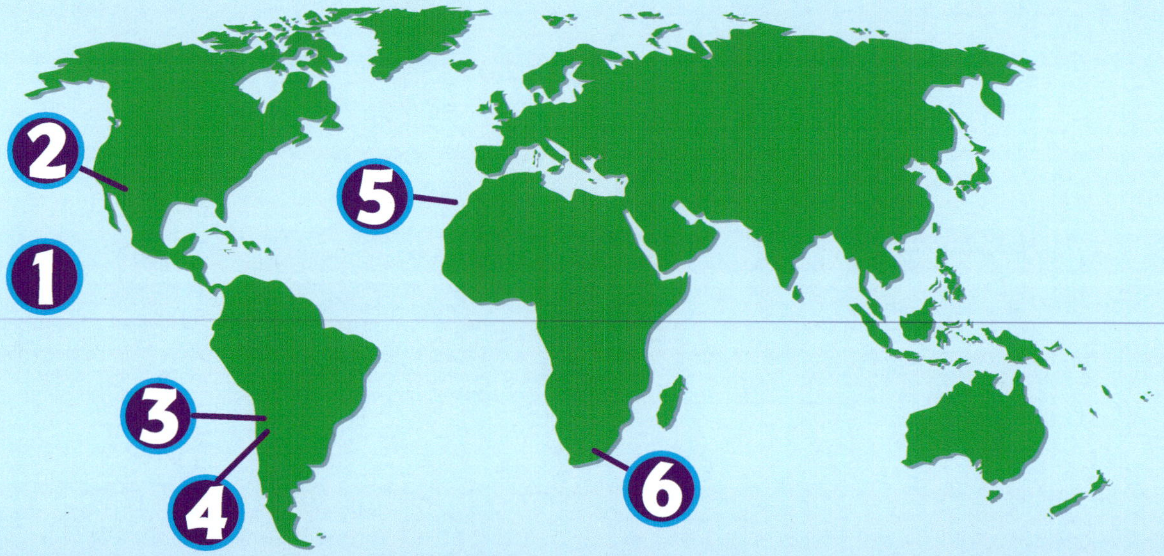

1 **Keck Observatory**
Mauna Kea, Hawaii, U.S.

2 **LBT (Large Binocular Telescope)**
Mount Graham, Arizona, U.S.

3 **Giant Magellan Telescope**
La Serena, Chile

4 **VLT (Very Large Telescope)**
Atacama Desert, Chile

5 **GTC (Great Canary Telescope)**
La Palma, Canary Islands

6 **SALT (South African Large Telescope)**
Sutherland, South Africa

Glossary

comet (KAH-muht) An object in space that travels around the sun. It's made of dust and gas, and sometimes forms a long, bright tail.

light-year (LYT–YIHR) A unit of length equal to how far light can travel in one year, about 6 trillion miles (9.7 trillion km).

magnify (MAAG-nuh-fy) To cause to appear larger.

medium (MEE-dee-uhm) Matter through which anything acts.

observatory (uhb-ZUHR-vuh-tohr-ee) A structure that has tools for studying the sun, moon, planets, and stars.

primary (PRY-mehr-ee) Main.

Index